To:

From:

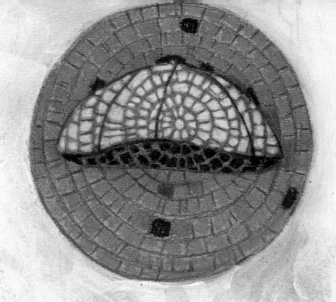

To my parishes, especially St. Catharine's of Pelham
and St. Joseph's of Yorkville —E. O.

To my mother and father —O. D.

BLOOMSBURY CHILDREN'S BOOKS
Bloomsbury Publishing Inc., part of Bloomsbury Publishing Plc
1385 Broadway, New York, NY 10018

BLOOMSBURY, BLOOMSBURY CHILDREN'S BOOKS, and the Diana logo are trademarks of Bloomsbury Publishing Plc

First published in the United States of America in September 2018 by Bloomsbury Children's Books

Bloomsbury books may be purchased for business or promotional use. For information on bulk
purchases please contact Macmillan Corporate and Premium Sales Department at specialmarkets@macmillan.com

Library of Congress Cataloging-in-Publication Data
Names: Otheguy, Emma, author. | Dominguez, Oliver, illustrator.
Title: Pope Francis : builder of bridges / by Emma Otheguy ; illustrated by Oliver Dominguez.
Description: New York : Bloomsbury, 2018. | Includes bibliographical references.
Identifiers: LCCN 2017052501 (print) • LCCN 2018005508 (e-book)
ISBN 978-1-68119-560-5 (hardcover) • ISBN 978-1-68119-561-2 (e-book) • ISBN 978-1-68119-562-9 (e-PDF)
Subjects: LCSH: Francis, Pope, 1936– —Juvenile literature.
Classification: LCC BX1378.7 .O84 2018 (print) | LCC BX1378.7 (e-book) | DDC 282.092 [B]—dc23
LC record available at https://lccn.loc.gov/2017052501

Art created with acrylic, gouache, watercolor, ink, and Prismacolor NuPastel on BFK Rives tan and cream paper
Typeset in Albertus MT • Book design by Danielle Ceccolini
Printed in China by Leo Paper Products, Heshan, Guangdong
2 4 6 8 10 9 7 5 3 1

All papers used by Bloomsbury Publishing Plc are natural, recyclable products made from wood grown in well-managed forests.
The manufacturing processes conform to the environmental regulations of the country of origin.

To find out more about our authors and books visit www.bloomsbury.com and sign up for our newsletters.

POPE FRANCIS

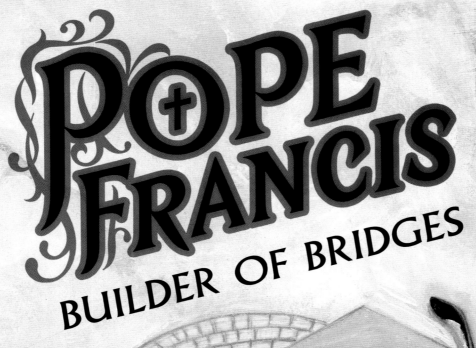

BUILDER OF BRIDGES

EMMA OTHEGUY
illustrated by OLIVER DOMINGUEZ

BLOOMSBURY
CHILDREN'S BOOKS
NEW YORK LONDON OXFORD NEW DELHI SYDNEY

As a child, Jorge Bergoglio would skip through the city of Buenos Aires alongside his grandma Rosa, keeping time with the street musicians' lively *milongas*, their tango-like songs. He jumped into games of pickup soccer, racing his friends for the ball, pumping his hands in the air, and dreaming of the **SMACK!** of a goal in a real live net.

Every day, Grandma Rosa taught Jorge how to pray.

They prayed together in the mornings and in the evenings. They prayed during Easter, when the streets were lined with processions, and they prayed at Christmas, when the city sparkled with color and light.

One day, Jorge noticed women on the street corner wearing hats and uniforms he'd never seen before. He tugged on Grandma Rosa's sleeve to ask why they were dressed that way.

Grandma Rosa pulled Jorge close to her and told him that the women were Protestant missionaries. They weren't Catholic like Jorge's family, but that didn't mean they weren't good.

Jorge watched the women a little longer. He was glad to know that anyone—of any faith—could be good.

As he grew older, Jorge wondered how *he* could be good and help others. He kept thinking about it as he sorted through the beakers and flasks at the chemistry lab where he worked as a young man. His father, who had come to Argentina from Italy in search of a better life, had taught him the importance of hard work, but his grandma Rosa had shown him that the most important work was to help others. Jorge longed to do that work.

The more he explored Buenos Aires, the more Jorge noticed people suffering. Some were so poor that they lived in the *villas miserias*, the miserable slums.

Each day in his prayers, Jorge remembered the poor and asked for a way to help.

In the stories of long-ago saints, Jorge found inspiration. He wanted to be like Saint Thérèse of Lisieux, sweet and gentle; or like Saint Francis of Assisi, who had given all his gold and silver to the poor. Saint Francis had helped even the smallest of animals, because he said that every living thing, rich or poor, human or animal, needed love.

Jorge found his path in a group of priests who expressed their love and care by teaching in schools around the world. He lived and worked with this group, the Jesuits, while he studied the Bible. When he was in his thirties, Jorge became a priest himself, and was now called Father Bergoglio. His whole family celebrated—but no one was happier than Grandma Rosa!

As a priest, Father Bergoglio wanted to bring the kids in his neighborhood some of the fun of his own childhood. He hosted soccer games and movie nights, and on special occasions he gave the kids hot chocolate!

After years of work, Father Bergoglio became Bishop of Buenos Aires. He still remembered the *villas miserias*, the slums where children worried and suffered, but now he had a team of priests who worked with him to help entire families. He and the other priests sent kids to school, opened clinics to heal the sick, and visited grandparents if they were lonely.

Across Argentina, people began to call Father Bergoglio the "Slum Bishop" because of his role in the *villas miserias*. In Rome, Pope John Paul II heard about his work and named him a cardinal.

When Pope Benedict XVI resigned, Father Bergoglio flew to Rome to help choose the new pope. The cardinals gathered every day to talk about who would be the best leader, and some people wanted Father Bergoglio!

There had never been a pope from South America before, and there had never been a Jesuit pope. Some said there never would be.

For more than a week, the cardinals listened to speeches and prayed for inspiration. Finally, the time came to cast their votes.

On a rainy evening in March, crowds of faithful Catholics filled Saint Peter's Square, and around the world, on radios, on televisions, and on the internet, people tuned in to watch the chimney of the Sistine Chapel. Would the smoke that filled the sky be white or black?

In every corner of the globe, people cheered.

It was Father Bergoglio!

He greeted people in the square not as Jorge or Father Bergoglio, but with the new name he had chosen, like all popes do when they are elected. Father Bergoglio was now Pope Francis—a pope to welcome all God's people, like Saint Francis had done so long ago.

Because the saint had always dressed in simple clothing, Pope Francis refused to wear lavish garments, like golden crosses and elegant robes.

"If we are too attached to riches," he said, "we are not free."

It was almost Easter when Pope Francis was elected, and people around the world couldn't wait to see how he would celebrate the most holy week of the year.

On Holy Thursday, Pope Francis broke with tradition. Instead of celebrating in a church, he celebrated in a prison. Instead of washing only men's feet, Pope Francis kissed and washed the feet of women as well as men, and Muslims as well as Catholics.

"This is a symbol, it is a sign," Pope Francis told the prisoners. "Washing your feet means I am at your service."

Some Catholics were amazed, but another word for pope is "pontiff"— a person who builds bridges for everyone, no matter who they are.

As the water poured forth from the pitcher, a bit of hope sparked in Catholics' hearts.

Pope Francis had many new responsibilities now, but he kept extending his bridges to reach more and more people.

He traveled to an island off the coast of Italy, where Muslim refugees had tried to escape wars and hunger on rafts. Pope Francis wanted refugees to find new opportunities, like his parents had found when they left Italy for Argentina.

"These our brothers and sisters seek to leave difficult situations in order to find a little serenity and peace," he told the crowds. "They seek a better place for themselves and for their families."

The pontiff lowered a decorated wreath into the sea, and he prayed that those in need of a new home would always find a bridge for the journey and an open door at its end.

More people are left homeless and in need as the planet heats, the oceans overflow, and farms and forests disappear. Near Francis's own Argentina, ranchers chop down the trees of the Amazon rain forest, destroying the habitats of animals and humans alike.

Pope Francis feels the *crack* of those falling trees in his own heart.

"Creation is a gift, it is a wonderful gift that God has given us, so that we care for it and we use it for the benefit of all, always with great respect and gratitude," he said.

In a letter to every bishop in the world, he explained that we can't hog or hoard earth's gifts: we all have to protect the planet, so that we can all share its plenty.

The pontiff builds bridges to ordinary people, especially children. Sometimes he stops his popemobile to joke with people around Rome or to kiss a baby's head. When his favorite team wins a soccer match, Pope Francis whoops and cheers!

Every year, Pope Francis invites kids in need to visit him on a Children's Train. He talks to the kids in an easygoing style. Instead of just preaching, Pope Francis asks the kids questions and encourages them to speak up. One year, the children brought kites on board, as a reminder that they could soar above.

With laughter, prayer, and well-chosen words, the pontiff proclaims that each and every living thing shares the same planet, the same love: and love always builds bridges.

AUTHOR'S NOTE

Pope Francis once described the Roman Catholic Church as a house with the doors thrown open. I think of Pope Francis as the man grasping the handle, pushing against the wood with his shoulder. The door to the Church sometimes sticks, but Pope Francis has moved toward a culture of social justice, care for the needy, and acceptance of all peoples.

I think Pope Francis might identify with my earliest experiences of the Church, as a child in a large Latinx family. Catholic holidays in my house were celebrated with music, dancing, and, above all, family—which, to my parents, seemed to mean anyone and everyone they could find. I came to associate Catholicism with a sense of abundance: abundant food and drink, abundant conversation, and an abundance of space in our hearts for siblings, cousins, and friends. Our Catholicism wasn't quiet or solemn—it was always mixed with the popular piety of the Caribbean; with chaotic banter in English and Spanish; and with shrieks, giggles, and laughter. The joy and lightness that Pope Francis brings to the pontificate highlight how important such an environment can be to Catholic life. When Pope Francis talks about the Church as a house, I see his childhood home in Buenos Aires, or mine in New York—vibrant places, overflowing with family.

As I grew up, my relationship with the Church expanded to include our parish in the suburbs of New York City. I came to love the quiet stillness of this small, dark church, as well as the guitar music and sunlight of the churches I visited with family in Miami and Puerto Rico. The Church became a link between the Latinx culture of my family and the cultures I experienced outside of home. Through sacrament, my life was tied to that of my beloved godmother, a German Catholic who survived World War II, married a Jewish refugee, and moved to New York City, where she became an essential part of our Latinx family. The Church I knew as a kid was a place of acceptance—a haven and spiritual home for refugees.

Many people today do not experience the accepting culture I enjoyed in the Church, but I join other Catholics in my hope that Pope Francis's papacy is a step toward the Church as it is truly meant to be: a house filled with family, with music and dancing, with the clatter of many languages, and with its doors forever open to the world.

TIMELINE

1936
Jorge Mario Bergoglio is born in Buenos Aires, Argentina.

1950
Jorge Bergoglio enters the Escuela Nacional de Educación Técnica, where he studies to be a chemical technician.

1958
Jorge Bergoglio enters novitiate, or training, to become a Jesuit priest.

1969
Jorge Bergoglio is ordained as a priest.

1992
Father Bergoglio is appointed Bishop of Buenos Aires.

2001
Father Bergoglio is named a cardinal.

2013
Father Bergoglio is elected pope.

2013
Pope Francis washes the feet of twelve prisoners, including women and Muslims.

2013
Pope Francis lays a wreath on the Mediterranean Sea in honor of North African refugees.

2015
Pope Francis publishes an encyclical, a letter to the bishops, about the environment called *Laudato si': On Care for Our Common Home.*

2018
Pope Francis turns his focus to the plight of refugees all over the world.

GLOSSARY

BISHOP: A priest who oversees many churches in one region. The region the bishop oversees is called a diocese. Bishops are also responsible for ordaining new priests.

CARDINAL: A bishop who helps elect and advise the pope.

JESUIT: The Jesuits are an order, or group, of Catholic priests and brothers. Unlike parish priests, Jesuits usually don't work for a specific church. Instead, they are best known as educators, and often teach in schools and universities. The Jesuit Order dates back to the sixteenth century and is also called the Society of Jesus.

MILONGA: A type of music that is related to tango. "Milonga" also refers to a style of ballroom dance popular in Argentina.

ORDINATION: A sacramental act in which someone becomes a priest.

POPE: The leader of the Roman Catholic Church and the Bishop of Rome.

SAINT PETER'S SQUARE: A public square outside the pope's headquarters in Rome. People standing in the square can see the smoke rising from the Sistine Chapel when a new pope is elected.

SISTINE CHAPEL: The chapel in Rome where the cardinals meet to vote on the new pope. During the election, a chimney is installed inside the chapel. If the cardinals vote but don't get the two-thirds majority needed to elect a pope, they send black smoke up the chimney. Once they've elected a new pope, they send up white smoke.

SWISS GUARDS: The Swiss Guards are responsible for keeping the pope safe. Some Swiss Guards wear blue, red, orange, and yellow uniforms, although others wear simpler clothing.

VATICAN CITY: Vatican City is both a city and a country. It is located in Rome, Italy, making it a city within a city. Since the fourteenth century, most popes have lived in the Vatican.

YERBA MATE: A naturally caffeinated drink that can be consumed hot or cold. It is the national drink of Argentina, and it is usually drunk out of a special cup and straw called a gourd and bombilla. Yerba mate is one of Pope Francis's favorites.

ZUCCHETTO: A simple skullcap worn by Catholic priests.

SELECTED BIBLIOGRAPHY

Allen, John L., Jr. "Francis: The Pope's Bold Message Comes to America." *Time Magazine*, special edition, 2015.

Allen, John L., Jr. "Pope Francis Gets his 'Oxygen' from the Slums." *National Catholic Reporter*, April 7, 2013. https://www.ncronline.org/blogs/francis-chronicles/pope-francis-gets-his-oxygen-slums.

Bermúdez, Alejandro, ed. and trans. *Pope Francis: Our Brother, Our Friend; Personal Recollections about the Man Who Became Pope*. San Francisco: Ignatius Press, 2013.

O'Kane, Lydia. "Pope: Open the Door to Faith." Vatican Radio, May 25, 2013. http://en.radiovaticana.va/storico/2013/05/25/pope_open_the_door_to_faith/en1-695466.

Piqué, Elisabetta. *Pope Francis: Life and Revolution; A Biography of Jorge Bergoglio*. Translated by Anna Mazzotti and Lydia Colin. Chicago: Loyola Press, 2013. Originally published as *Francisco. Vida y revolución* (Buenos Aires, Argentina: Editorial El Ateneo, 2013).

Rubin, Sergio, and Francesca Ambrogetti. *Pope Francis: Conversations with Jorge Bergoglio*. Translated by Laura Dail Literary Agency. New York: G. P. Putnam's Sons, 2010. Originally published as *El Jesuita: Conversaciones con Jorge Bergoglio* (Buenos Aires, Argentina: Ediciones B Argentina S.A., 2010).

Scammell, Rosie. "Pope Francis to Greet Children of Prisoners with a Train Ride and a Gift of Kites." *Washington Post*, May 29, 2015. https://www.washingtonpost.com/national/religion/pope-francis-to-greet-children-of-prisoners-with-a-train-ride-and-a-gift-of-kites/2015/05/29/1332726c-0635-11e5-93f4-f24d4af7f97d_story.html?utm_term=.a945bea0779e.

The Telegraph. "Pope's Handwritten Notes of 2013 Speech to Cardinals Now Published," March 17, 2017. http://www.telegraph.co.uk/news/2017/03/17/popes-handwritten-notes-2013-speech-cardinals-now-published/.

Vallely, Paul. *Pope Francis: Untying the Knots; The Struggle for the Soul of Catholicism*, 2nd ed. New York: Bloomsbury, 2015.

Yardley, Jim. "A Humble Pope, Challenging the World." *New York Times*, September 18, 2015. https://www.nytimes.com/2015/09/19/world/europe/pope-francis.html.

QUOTATION SOURCES

PAGE 28

"If we are too attached to riches, we are not free."
Jorge Bergoglio, Twitter post, March 5, 2015, 12:30 a.m. https://twitter.com/pontifex/status/573400086572498944?lang=en.

PAGE 31

"This is a symbol, it is a sign.... Washing your feet means I am at your service."
Jorge Bergoglio, Homily, Rome, Italy, March 28, 2013. Transcribed and translated by Vatican Radio. Uebbing, David. "'I Do This with My Heart,' Pope Says Before Washing Inmates' Feet." Catholic News Agency, March 28, 2013. https://www.catholicnewsagency.com/news/i-do-this-with-my-heart-pope-says-before-washing-inmates-feet.

PAGE 32

"These our brothers and sisters seek to leave difficult situations in order to find a little serenity and peace. They seek a better place for themselves and for their families."
Jorge Bergoglio, Homily, Lampedusa, Italy, July 8, 2013. Transcribed and translated by Vatican Radio. *Houston Catholic Worker*, "Pope Francis Made His First Trip Outside the Vatican to Visit Migrants," September–October 2013, Vol. XXXIV, No. 4. https://cjd.org/2013/10/02/pope-francis-made-his-first-trip-outside-the-vatican-to-visit-migrants/.

PAGE 34

"Creation is a gift, it is a wonderful gift that God has given us, so that we care for it and we use it for the benefit of all, always with great respect and gratitude."
Jorge Bergoglio, General Audience, Vatican City, May 21, 2014. Transcribed and translated by Vatican Radio. Roewe, Brian. "Francis: Caring for the Earth a Thank-You Note to God." *Eco Catholic* (blog). *National Catholic Reporter*, May 22, 2014. https://www.ncronline.org/blogs/eco-catholic/francis-caring-earth-thank-you-note-god.

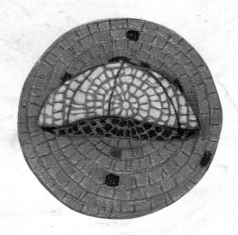

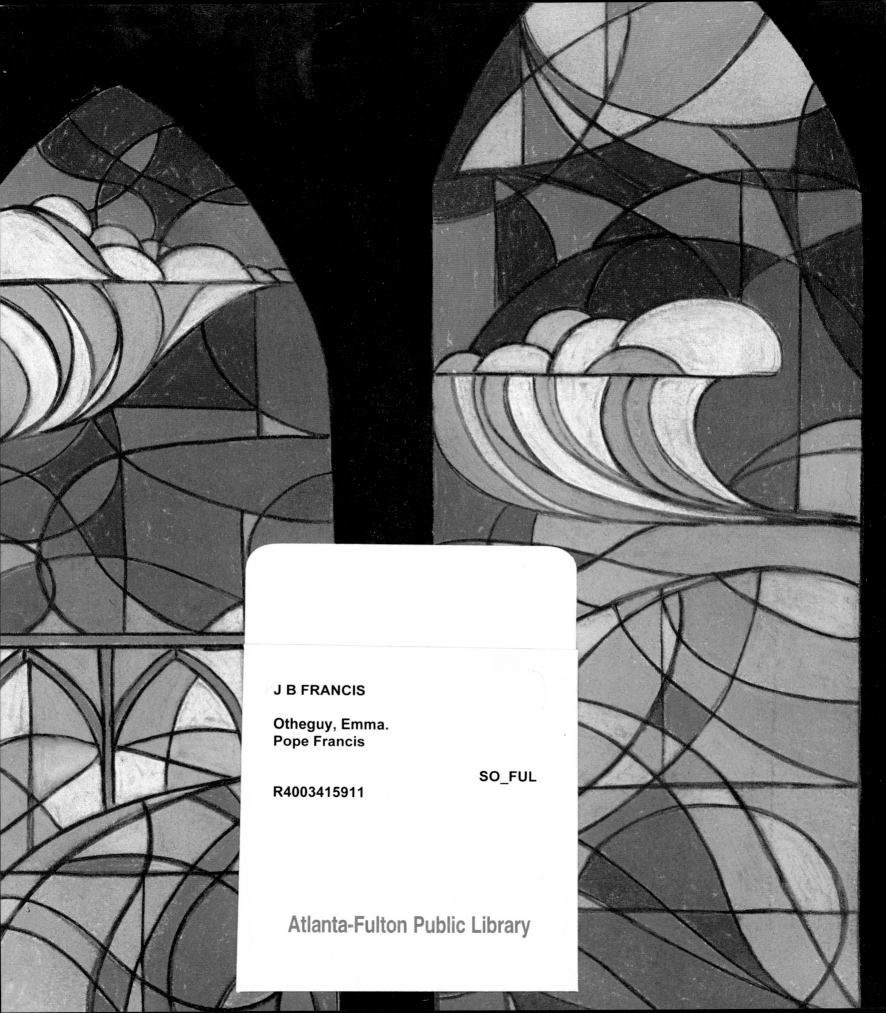